SECOND APRIL

and

THE BUCK IN THE SNOW

SECOND APRIL

and

The BUCK in the SNOW

By

EDNA ST. VINCENT MILLAY

With an Introduction by

WILLIAM ROSE BENÉT

New York

HARPER & BROTHERS PUBLISHERS

INTRODUCTION

By William Rose Benét

It may be over-obvious to point out that the effectively art-less is always due to art, just as spontaneity in a style does not imply easy writing. You will discover very soon that Miss Millay's most simple phrase and epithet are precise, and often not merely precise but memorable. Of late years, in a fever of experimentation, sight has been lost of the memo-rable phrase. But it is the True North of poetry. And if you have thrown away your compass, you may not be able to find your way out of the wood of words. Miss Millay has blazed her own trails too, in her time, but took along a wiz-ardly and silver-ringing axe to the clearing.

There is no mistaking the birthright of this poet. You will find her again and again speaking in no uncertain tones of her love for the coast of Maine. You will notice, as in all her references to nature, the thoroughly acquainted particu-larity with which she describes the places she knows. She is as exact as was Tennyson in her observation of familiar things—and despite the superciliousness of the uninformed, that is high praise. Let me illustrate through a few in-stances: ". . . the rain that flattens on the bay/ And the eel-grass in the cove"; "Still will the tamaracks be raining/ After the rain has ceased, . . ."; ". . . a useless wagon/ Standing beside some tumbled shed"; "White with daisies

v

and red with sorrel"; ". . . the soft shock/ Of wizened apples falling"; of a train, ". . . I see its cinders red on the sky,/ And hear its engine steaming"; rocks "slimed beneath to a beautiful green"; "If I could hear the green piles groaning."—all of that stanza from "Exile." You will find many others.

She was born in 1892 in Rockland, Maine. Before she was twenty she had written a remarkable long poem, "Renascence," which appeared in a prize-competition anthology in 1912, queerly enough not winning the prize. Her first book, *Renascence and Other Poems,* was published five years later, the year she graduated from Vassar. As a semiphilosophical poem, "Renascence" still stands up pretty well, even though early influences are apparent. One could recognize at once that an unusual poet was in the making. After *A Few Figs from Thistles* in 1920, in which with delight she detonated a few squibs under the skirts of Mrs. Grundy, the best of Miss Millay's earlier books, *Second April,* followed in 1921. You have it here, along with a later. May I point out in it the perfection of the brief poem "Passer Mortuus Est"? Edna Millay would never have been content to remain a feminine Landor, but that poet, whose middle name (by the bye) was Savage, despite his inclination toward the Parian, would, I am sure, have approved those lines. On the facing page is a poem, "Weeds," with a last verse that might be envied by any poet, ending "The blood too bright, the brow accurst." Which is exactly what I mean when I speak of Miss Millay's gift for memorable phrase.

A good many extraordinary poets retain childlikeness—

not to be confused with childishness. William Blake, in his *Songs of Innocence,* was such. Miss Millay shows this characteristic in "The Blue-Flag in the Bog" and "The Bean-Stalk." You will find it again in the italicized lines of the poem "Low-Tide," a poem of considerable depth, though seemingly so simple. But may I also point to another fine quality in this poet's work: She has always been a rebel. She is on the side of her natural world against the incumbent universes. In "The Blue-Flag," the verse that suddenly strikes fire—after "And I slipped away like water/ Through the fingers of the blest!"—is, in the description of "that tall blue flower":

> On its roots like iron claws
> Rearing up so blue and tall,—
> It was all the gallant Earth
> With its back against a wall!

She has "the scorn of scorn" as well as "the love of love," such as was supposed, by a great singer of an elder day, to be the true inheritance of the poet. She calls Death all sorts of names also. She remains unreconciled to the termination of existence. "Moriturus," the opening poem of *The Buck in the Snow,* although admirable in its dexterity, has for me rather too scolding a quality. Yet even here one can admire Miss Millay's masterful use of the familiar reference and the colloquial expression. But set it beside John Donne's sonnet beginning "Death, be not proud . . ." and it does not fare so well. This is, perhaps, to compare two incomparables, and we are immediately outfaced by Miss Millay's own sonnets, in which she does indeed challenge the best verse of three centuries and a half ago, to wit of the age of Shakespeare. The next to last poem in *Second April,* the sonnet beginning, "Cherish you then the hope . . ." opens this challenge. It is the best of a sequence of a dozen, the first of which begins with an indifferent octave but culminates in four surprising lines. We begin to be aware of her strength as well as of her skill; of her ability to write poems of more than charm, beautiful and touching as may be such love poems as "Elaine" and "Mariposa," fine and somehow Greek as is "Assault," stately as is the "Ode to Silence" which still, to me, does not quite seem to be as complete in itself as most of her individual work.

Two years after *Second April* came *The Harp Weaver and Other Poems.* The title poem is one of her best ballads. This book won her the Pulitzer Prize in 1923, and it confirmed beyond peradventure her dedication to poetry, declared so passionately in the twelfth sonnet of the earlier sequence. Here were sonnets of an intensity unknown since the time of Elizabeth Barrett Browning, though of a new vintage wholly.

In this year Edna St. Vincent Millay married Eugen Jan Boissevain, who rendered to her a devotion—and not only a devotion, but an understanding of the demands of her art —that endured until his death in 1949. Two years after their marriage they repaired to farmland in upper New York, in the Berkshires on the Massachusetts border. The place was Austerlitz, their farm known as Steepletop. Miss Millay has lived there ever since, with excursions abroad and to other places in her own country.

The Buck in the Snow appeared five years later, after she

viii

had written the libretto, *The King's Henchman,* the love story being of Saxon England, for an opera by Deems Taylor which was produced at the Metropolitan Opera House in New York.

I have already spoken of the opening poem of this book of poems. Again we find her genuine gift in it for describing natural things precisely. "The Bobolink" might seem, as a subject, worthy only of the most sentimental kind of long-bearded verse, but here is a new poem on that long-suffering bird that springs from acute observation, conveys genuine mirth, and contains so memorable a line as

In the shadow of the hawk we feather our nests.

There is always the characteristic Millay touch. In "The Hawkweed," for instance:

And blest be Beauty, that enchants
The frail, the solitary lance.

In "Northern April" we have, "The soft antiphonal speech of the doubled brook"; in "There at Dusk. . . ," "the dumb white nicotine awakes and utters her fragrance"; and in "Mist in the Valley" we are reminded once more of that nostalgia for the sea from her who had

built me a house on upland acres,
Sweet with the pinxter, bright and rough
With the rusty blackbird long before the winter's done,
But smelling never of bayberry hot in the sun,
Nor ever loud with the pounding of the long white
breakers,—

I can appreciate that particularly, as five months of the year I know that smell of bayberry, and the Equinox brings the long white breakers to pound beneath my study window. When Edna St. Vincent Millay speaks of a hardy garden, or of pigeons, or of a buck and his doe in the apple orchard, she is never writing for effect, she is writing of the thing seen and known, observed with the extortionate eye of the true poet.

And in this book her rebel instinct takes fire again from a dark miscarriage of justice. For some time, when called upon to read from her poems in public, she insisted upon including her "Justice Denied in Massachusetts," dealing with the case of Sacco and Vanzetti. The poems that follow, in part two of the book, end with a quatrain *aere perennius*:

To Those Without Pity

Cruel of heart, lay down my song.
Your reading eyes have done me wrong.
Not for you was the pen bitten,
And the mind wrung, and the song written.

Whatever of archness may seem somewhat too much to sweeten the earlier work is long gone. And "Dirge Without Music" is a nobler poem about death than "Moriturus." I remember hearing Miss Millay's own voice reading in her room at Steepletop to two hushed listeners her great sonnet "On Hearing a Symphony of Beethoven."

The title taken from a poem in this volume, "Wine from These Grapes" appeared upon a book in 1934, but it was three years preceded by a distinguished sonnet cycle, *Fatal Interview,* in which are some of Miss Millay's greatest poems. *Conversation at Midnight,* in 1937, was a daring experiment in another *genre*. Other books followed. Her

Collected Sonnets were published in 1941, and the *Collected Lyrics* in 1943.

I have omitted her early concern with the theater, which expressed itself not only in acting in youth with the Provincetown Players, but also in several short (and one long) satirical fantasies akin to poetry. No one who ever knew her could fail to recognize her talent for the stage which was overborne by her greater and consuming thirst for poetry.

I present these remarks as quite inadequate. Youth will find its own way through her work, and nothing would give her greater pleasure than the intelligent attention of youth. What her wisest word to you would be I do not know, but to herself, as she came to attain the stature of one of the greatest poets of our time, it was in these unforgettable lines:

> Have done with blossoms for a time, be bare;
> Split rock, plunge downward; take heroic soil;
> Deeper than bones—no pasture for you there;
> Deeper than water, deeper than gold and oil:
> Earth's fiery core alone can feed the bough
> That blooms between Orion and the Plough.

———

William Rose Benét is well known as a poet and critic. A native New Yorker, he was educated at the Sheffield Scientific School (Yale) and has received honorary degrees from Yale and from Dickinson College. In 1920, after years of editorial work and free-lancing, Mr. Benét helped found the Saturday Review of Literature *as associate editor, which position he still holds. He was awarded a Pulitzer Prize for his autobiographical verse novel,* The Dust Which Is God *(1941). Among his other volumes of poetry are* Merchants from Cathay *(1913),* The Burglar of the Zodiac *(1918),* Moons of Grandeur *(1920),* Man Possessed *(1927), and* The Stairway of Surprise *(1947). He has edited several notable anthologies of prose and verse; among the more recent is* The Poetry of Freedom *(1948).*

SECOND APRIL

CONTENTS

SPRING

To what purpose, April, do you return again?
Beauty is not enough.
You can no longer quiet me with the redness
Of little leaves opening stickily.
I know what I know.
The sun is hot on my neck as I observe
The spikes of the crocus.
The smell of the earth is good.
It is apparent that there is no death.
But what does that signify?
Not only under ground are the brains of men
Eaten by maggots.
Life in itself
Is nothing,
An empty cup, a flight of uncarpeted stairs.
It is not enough that yearly, down this hill,
April
Comes like an idiot, babbling and strewing flowers.

CITY TREES

The trees along this city street,
　　Save for the traffic and the trains,
Would make a sound as thin and sweet
　　As trees in country lanes.

And people standing in their shade
　　Out of a shower, undoubtedly
Would hear such music as is made
　　Upon a country tree.

Oh, little leaves that are so dumb
　　Against the shrieking city air,
I watch you when the wind has come,—
　　I know what sound is there.

THE BLUE-FLAG IN THE BOG

God had called us, and we came;
  Our loved Earth to ashes left;
Heaven was a neighbor's house,
  Open flung to us, bereft.

Gay the lights of Heaven showed,
  And 'twas God who walked ahead;
Yet I wept along the road,
  Wanting my own house instead.

Wept unseen, unheeded cried,
  "All you things my eyes have kissed,
Fare you well! We meet no more,
  Lovely, lovely tattered mist!

Weary wings that rise and fall
  All day long above the fire!"—
Red with heat was every wall,
  Rough with heat was every wire—

"Fare you well, you little winds
  That the flying embers chase!
Fare you well, you shuddering day,
  With your hands before your face!

And, ah, blackened by strange blight,
  Or to a false sun unfurled,
Now forevermore goodbye,
  All the gardens in the world!

On the windless hills of Heaven,
  That I have no wish to see,
White, eternal lilies stand,
  By a lake of ebony.

But the Earth forevermore
  Is a place where nothing grows,—
Dawn will come, and no bud break;
  Evening, and no blossom close.

Spring will come, and wander slow
    Over an indifferent land,
Stand beside an empty creek,
    Hold a dead seed in her hand."

God had called us, and we came,
    But the blessed road I trod
Was a bitter road to me,
    And at heart I questioned God.

"Though in Heaven," I said, "be all
    That the heart would most desire,
Held Earth naught save souls of sinners
    Worth the saving from a fire?

Withered grass,—the wasted growing!
    Aimless ache of laden boughs!"
Little things God had forgotten
    Called me, from my burning house.

"Though in Heaven," I said, "be all
   That the eye could ask to see,
All the things I ever knew
   Are this blaze in back of me."

"Though in Heaven," I said, "be all
   That the ear could think to lack,
All the things I ever knew
   Are this roaring at my back."

It was God who walked ahead,
   Like a shepherd to the fold;
In his footsteps fared the weak,
   And the weary and the old,

Glad enough of gladness over,
   Ready for the peace to be,—
But a thing God had forgotten
   Was the growing bones of me.

And I drew a bit apart,
  And I lagged a bit behind,
And I thought on Peace Eternal,
  Lest He look into my mind:

And I gazed upon the sky,
  And I thought of Heavenly Rest,—
And I slipped away like water
  Through the fingers of the blest!

All their eyes were fixed on Glory,
  Not a glance brushed over me;
"Alleluia! Alleluia!"
  Up the road,—and I was free.

And my heart rose like a freshet,
  And it swept me on before,
Giddy as a whirling stick,
  Till I felt the earth once more.

All the Earth was charred and black,
　Fire had swept from pole to pole;
And the bottom of the sea
　Was as brittle as a bowl;

And the timbered mountain-top
　Was as naked as a skull,—
Nothing left, nothing left,
　Of the Earth so beautiful!

"Earth," I said, "how can I leave you?"
　"You are all I have," I said;
"What is left to take my mind up,
　Living always, and you dead?"

"Speak!" I said, "Oh, tell me something!
　Make a sign that I can see!
For a keepsake! To keep always!
　Quick!—before God misses me!"

And I listened for a voice;—
　　But my heart was all I heard;
Not a screech-owl, not a loon,
　　Not a tree-toad said a word.

And I waited for a sign;—
　　Coals and cinders, nothing more;
And a little cloud of smoke
　　Floating on a valley floor.

And I peered into the smoke
　　Till it rotted, like a fog:—
There, encompassed round by fire,
　　Stood a blue-flag in a bog!

Little flames came wading out,
　　Straining, straining towards its stem,
But it was so blue and tall
　　That it scorned to think of them!

Red and thirsty were their tongues,
  As the tongues of wolves must be,
But it was so blue and tall—
  Oh, I laughed, I cried, to see!

All my heart became a tear,
  All my soul became a tower,
Never loved I anything
  As I loved that tall blue flower!

It was all the little boats
  That had ever sailed the sea,
It was all the little books
  That had gone to school with me;

On its roots like iron claws
  Rearing up so blue and tall,—
It was all the gallant Earth
  With its back against a wall!

In a breath, ere I had breathed,—
    Oh, I laughed, I cried, to see!—
I was kneeling at its side,
    And it leaned its head on me!

Crumbling stones and sliding sand
    Is the road to Heaven now;
Icy at my straining knees
    Drags the awful under-tow;

Soon but stepping-stones of dust
    Will the road to Heaven be,—
Father, Son and Holy Ghost,
    Reach a hand and rescue me!

"There—there, my blue-flag flower;
    Hush—hush—go to sleep;
That is only God you hear,
    Counting up His folded sheep!

Lullabye—lullabye—
    That is only God that calls,
Missing me, seeking me,
    Ere the road to nothing falls!

He will set His mighty feet
    Firmly on the sliding sand;
Like a little frightened bird
    I will creep into His hand;

I will tell Him all my grief,
    I will tell Him all my sin;
He will give me half His robe
    For a cloak to wrap you in.

Lullabye—lullabye—"
    Rocks the burnt-out planet free!—
Father, Son and Holy Ghost,
    Reach a hand and rescue me!

Ah, the voice of love at last!
  Lo, at last the face of light!
And the whole of His white robe
  For a cloak against the night!

And upon my heart asleep
  All the things I ever knew!—
"Holds Heaven not some cranny, Lord,
  For a flower so tall and blue?"

All's well and all's well!
  Gay the lights of Heaven show!
In some moist and Heavenly place
  We will set it out to grow.

JOURNEY

Ah, could I lay me down in this long grass
And close my eyes, and let the quiet wind
Blow over me—I am so tired, so tired
Of passing pleasant places! All my life,
Following Care along the dusty road,
Have I looked back at loveliness and sighed;
Yet at my hand an unrelenting hand
Tugged ever, and I passed. All my life long
Over my shoulder have I looked at peace;
And now I fain would lie in this long grass
And close my eyes.
                                    Yet onward!

                                                Cat birds call
Through the long afternoon, and creeks at dusk
Are guttural. Whip-poor-wills wake and cry,
Drawing the twilight close about their throats.
Only my heart makes answer. Eager vines
Go up the rocks and wait; flushed apple-trees
Pause in their dance and break the ring for me;
Dim, shady wood-roads, redolent of fern
And bayberry, that through sweet bevies thread

14

Of round-faced roses, pink and petulant,
Look back and beckon ere they disappear.
Only my heart, only my heart responds.
Yet, ah, my path is sweet on either side
All through the dragging day,—sharp underfoot
And hot, and like dead mist the dry dust hangs—
But far, oh, far as passionate eye can reach,
And long, ah, long as rapturous eye can cling,
The world is mine: blue hill, still silver lake,
Broad field, bright flower, and the long white road
A gateless garden, and an open path:
My feet to follow, and my heart to hold.

EEL-GRASS

No matter what I say,
  All that I really love
Is the rain that flattens on the bay,
  And the eel-grass in the cove;
The jingle-shells that lie and bleach
  At the tide-line, and the trace
Of higher tides along the beach:
  Nothing in this place.

ELEGY BEFORE DEATH

THERE will be rose and rhododendron
  When you are dead and under ground;
Still will be heard from white syringas
  Heavy with bees, a sunny sound;

Still will the tamaracks be raining
  After the rain has ceased, and still
Will there be robins in the stubble,
  Brown sheep upon the warm green hill.

Spring will not ail nor autumn falter;
  Nothing will know that you are gone,
Saving alone some sullen plough-land
  None but yourself sets foot upon;

Saving the may-weed and the pig-weed
  Nothing will know that you are dead,—
These, and perhaps a useless wagon
  Standing beside some tumbled shed.

Oh, there will pass with your great passing

Little of beauty not your own,—
Only the light from common water,
Only the grace from simple stone!

THE BEAN-STALK

Ho, Giant! This is I!
I have built me a bean-stalk into your sky!
La,—but it's lovely, up so high!

This is how I came,—I put
Here my knee, there my foot,
Up and up, from shoot to shoot—
And the blessèd bean-stalk thinning
Like the mischief all the time,
Till it took me rocking, spinning,
In a dizzy, sunny circle,
Making angles with the root,
Far and out above the cackle
Of the city I was born in,
Till the little dirty city
In the light so sheer and sunny
Shone as dazzling bright and pretty
As the money that you find
In a dream of finding money—
What a wind! What a morning!—

Till the tiny, shiny city,
When I shot a glance below,
Shaken with a giddy laughter,
Sick and blissfully afraid,
Was a dew-drop on a blade,
And a pair of moments after
Was the whirling guess I made,—
And the wind was like a whip

Cracking past my icy ears,
And my hair stood out behind,
And my eyes were full of tears,
Wide-open and cold,
More tears than they could hold,
The wind was blowing so,
And my teeth were in a row,
Dry and grinning,
And I felt my foot slip,
And I scratched the wind and whined,
And I clutched the stalk and jabbered,
With my eyes shut blind,—
What a wind! What a wind!

Your broad sky, Giant,
Is the shelf of a cupboard;
I make bean-stalks, I'm
A builder, like yourself,
But bean-stalks is my trade,
I couldn't make a shelf,
Don't know how they're made,
Now, a bean-stalk is more pliant—
La, what a climb!

WEEDS

WHITE with daisies and red with sorrel
 And empty, empty under the sky!—
Life is a quest and love a quarrel—
 Here is a place for me to lie.

Daisies spring from damnèd seeds,
 And this red fire that here I see
Is a worthless crop of crimson weeds,
 Cursed by farmers thriftily.

But here, unhated for an hour,
 The sorrel runs in ragged flame,
The daisy stands, a bastard flower,
 Like flowers that bear an honest name.

And here a while, where no wind brings
 The baying of a pack athirst,
May sleep the sleep of blessèd things,
 The blood too bright, the brow accurst.

PASSER MORTUUS EST

DEATH devours all lovely things;
  Lesbia with her sparrow
Shares the darkness,—presently
  Every bed is narrow.

Unremembered as old rain
  Dries the sheer libation,
And the little petulant hand
  Is an annotation.

After all, my erstwhile dear,
  My no longer cherished,
Need we say it was not love,
  Now that love is perished?

PASTORAL

If it were only still!—
With far away the shrill
Crying of a cock;
Or the shaken bell
From a cow's throat
Moving through the bushes;
Or the soft shock
Of wizened apples falling
From an old tree
In a forgotten orchard
Upon the hilly rock!

Oh, grey hill,
Where the grazing herd
Licks the purple blossom,
Crops the spiky weed!
Oh, stony pasture,
Where the tall mullein
Stands up so sturdy
On its little seed!

ASSAULT

I

I HAD forgotten how the frogs must sound
After a year of silence, else I think
I should not so have ventured forth alone
At dusk upon this unfrequented road.

II

I am waylaid by Beauty. Who will walk
Between me and the crying of the frogs?
Oh, savage Beauty, suffer me to pass,
That am a timid woman, on her way
From one house to another!

TRAVEL

THE railroad track is miles away,
  And the day is loud with voices speaking,
Yet there isn't a train goes by all day
  But I hear its whistle shrieking.

All night there isn't a train goes by,
  Though the night is still for sleep and dreaming
But I see its cinders red on the sky,
  And hear its engine steaming.

My heart is warm with the friends I make,
  And better friends I'll not be knowing,
Yet there isn't a train I wouldn't take,
  No matter where it's going.

LOW-TIDE

THESE wet rocks where the tide has been,
    Barnacled white and weeded brown
And slimed beneath to a beautiful green,
    These wet rocks where the tide went down
Will show again when the tide is high
    Faint and perilous, far from shore,
No place to dream, but a place to die,—
    The bottom of the sea once more.
There was a child that wandered through
    A giant's empty house all day,—
House full of wonderful things and new,
    But no fit place for a child to play.

SONG OF A SECOND APRIL

APRIL this year, not otherwise
  Than April of a year ago,
Is full of whispers, full of sighs,
  Of dazzling mud and dingy snow;
  Hepaticas that pleased you so
Are here again, and butterflies.

There rings a hammering all day,
  And shingles lie about the doors;
In orchards near and far away
  The grey wood-pecker taps and bores;
  The men are merry at their chores,
And children earnest at their play.

The larger streams run still and deep,
  Noisy and swift the small brooks run
Among the mullein stalks the sheep
  Go up the hillside in the sun,
  Pensively,—only you are gone,
You that alone I cared to keep.

ROSEMARY

For the sake of some things
   That be now no more
I will strew rushes
   On my chamber-floor,
I will plant bergamot
   At my kitchen-door.

For the sake of dim things
   That were once so plain
I will set a barrel
   Out to catch the rain,
I will hang an iron pot
   On an iron crane.

Many things be dead and gone
   That were brave and gay;
For the sake of these things
   I will learn to say,
"An it please you, gentle sirs,"
   "Alack!" and "Well-a-day!"

THE POET AND HIS BOOK

Down, you mongrel, Death!
  Back into your kennel!
I have stolen breath
  In a stalk of fennel!
You shall scratch and you shall whine
  Many a night, and you shall worry
  Many a bone, before you bury
One sweet bone of mine!

When shall I be dead?
  When my flesh is withered,
And above my head
  Yellow pollen gathered
All the empty afternoon?
  When sweet lovers pause and wonder
  Who am I that lie thereunder,
Hidden from the moon?

This my personal death?—
  That my lungs be failing
To inhale the breath

Others are exhaling?
This my subtle spirit's end?—
　　Ah, when the thawed winter splashes
　　Over these chance dust and ashes,
Weep not me, my friend!

Me, by no means dead
　　In that hour, but surely
When this book, unread,
　　Rots to earth obscurely,
And no more to any breast,
　　Close against the clamorous swelling
　　Of the thing there is no telling,
Are these pages pressed!

When this book is mould,
　　And a book of many
Waiting to be sold
　　For a casual penny,
In a little open case,
　　In a street unclean and cluttered,
　　Where a heavy mud is spattered
From the passing drays,

Stranger, pause and look;
   From the dust of ages
 ift this little book,
   Turn the tattered pages,
Read me, do not let me die!
   Search the fading letters, finding
   Steadfast in the broken binding
All that once was I!

When these veins are weeds,
   When these hollowed sockets
Watch the rooty seeds
   Bursting down like rockets,
And surmise the spring again,
   Or, remote in that black cupboard,
   Watch the pink worms writhing upward
At the smell of rain,

Boys and girls that lie
   Whispering in the hedges,
Do not let me die,
   Mix me with your pledges;
Boys and girls that slowly walk

In the woods, and weep, and quarrel,
  Staring past the pink wild laurel,
Mix me with your talk,

Do not let me die!
  Farmers at your raking,
When the sun is high,
  While the hay is making,
When, along the stubble strewn,
  Withering on their stalks uneaten,
  Strawberries turn dark and sweeten
In the lapse of noon;

Shepherds on the hills,
  In the pastures, drowsing
To the tinkling bells
  Of the brown sheep browsing;
Sailors crying through the storm;
  Scholars at your study; hunters
  Lost amid the whirling winter's
Whiteness uniform;

33

Men that long for sleep;
    Men that wake and revel;—
If an old song leap
    To your senses' level
At such moments, may it be
    Sometimes, though a moment only,
    Some forgotten, quaint and homely
Vehicle of me!

Women at your toil,
    Women at your leisure
Till the kettle boil,
    Snatch of me your pleasure,
Where the broom-straw marks the leaf;
    Women quiet with your weeping
    Lest you wake a workman sleeping,
Mix me with your grief!

Boys and girls that steal
    From the shocking laughter
Of the old, to kneel
    By a dripping rafter
Under the discolored eaves,

34

Out of trunks with hingeless covers
   Lifting tales of saints and lovers,
Travelers, goblins, thieves,

Suns that shine by night,
   Mountains made from valleys,—
Bear me to the light,
   Flat upon your bellies
By the webby window lie,
   Where the little flies are crawling,—
   Read me, margin me with scrawling,
Do not let me die!

Sexton, ply your trade!
   In a shower of gravel
Stamp upon your spade!
   Many a rose shall ravel,
Many a metal wreath shall rust
   In the rain, and I go singing
   Through the lots where you are flinging
Yellow clay on dust!

ALMS

My heart is what it was before,
  A house where people come and go;
But it is winter with your love,
  The sashes are beset with snow.

I light the lamp and lay the cloth,
  I blow the coals to blaze again;
But it is winter with your love,
  The frost is thick upon the pane.

I know a winter when it comes:
  The leaves are listless on the boughs;
I watched your love a little while,
  And brought my plants into the house.

I water them and turn them south,
  I snap the dead brown from the stem;
But it is winter with your love,—
  I only tend and water them.

There was a time I stood and watched
   The small, ill-natured sparrows' fray;
I loved the beggar that I fed,
   I cared for what he had to say,

I stood and watched him out of sight;
   Today I reach around the door
And set a bowl upon the step;
   My heart is what it was before,

But it is winter with your love;
   I scatter crumbs upon the sill,
And close the window,—and the birds
   May take or leave them, as they will.

INLAND

PEOPLE that build their houses inland,
  People that buy a plot of ground
Shaped like a house, and build a house there,
  Far from the sea-board, far from the sound

Of water sucking the hollow ledges,
  Tons of water striking the shore,—
What do they long for, as I long for
  One salt smell of the sea once more?

People the waves have not awakened,
  Spanking the boats at the harbor's head,
What do they long for, as I long for,—
  Starting up in my inland bed,

Beating the narrow walls, and finding
  Neither a window nor a door,
Screaming to God for death by drowning,—
  One salt taste of the sea once more?

TO A POET THAT DIED YOUNG

Minstrel, what have you to do
With this man that, after you,
Sharing not your happy fate,
Sat as England's Laureate?
Vainly, in these iron days,
Strives the poet in your praise,
Minstrel, by whose singing side
Beauty walked, until you died.

Still, though none should hark again,
Drones the blue-fly in the pane,
Thickly crusts the blackest moss,
Blows the rose its musk across,
Floats the boat that is forgot
None the less to Camelot.

Many a bard's untimely death
Lends unto his verses breath;
Here's a song was never sung:
Growing old is dying young.
Minstrel, what is this to you:

That a man you never knew,
When your grave was far and green,
Sat and gossipped with a queen?

Thalia knows how rare a thing
Is it, to grow old and sing;
When a brown and tepid tide
Closes in on every side.
Who shall say if Shelley's gold
Had withstood it to grow old?

WRAITH

"Thin Rain, whom are you haunting,
   That you haunt my door?"
—Surely it is not I she's wanting;
   Someone living here before—
"Nobody's in the house but me:
You may come in if you like and see."

Thin as thread, with exquisite fingers,—
   Have you seen her, any of you?—
Grey shawl, and leaning on the wind,
   And the garden showing through?

Glimmering eyes,—and silent, mostly,
   Sort of a whisper, sort of a purr,
Asking something, asking it over,
   If you get a sound from her.—

Ever see her, any of you?—
   Strangest thing I've ever known,—
Every night since I moved in,
   And I came to be alone.

"Thin Rain, hush with your knocking!
  You may not come in!
This is I that you hear rocking;
  Nobody's with me, nor has been!"

Curious, how she tried the window,—
  Odd, the way she tries the door,—
Wonder just what sort of people
  Could have had this house before . . .

EBB

I KNOW what my heart is like
    Since your love died:
It is like a hollow ledge
Holding a little pool
    Left there by the tide,
    A little tepid pool,
Drying inward from the edge.

ELAINE

Oh, come again to Astolat!
   I will not ask you to be kind.
And you may go when you will go,
   And I will stay behind.

I will not say how dear you are,
   Or ask you if you hold me dear,
Or trouble you with things for you
   The way I did last year.

So still the orchard, Lancelot,
   So very still the lake shall be,
You could not guess—though you should guess—
   What is become of me.

So wide shall be the garden-walk,
   The garden-seat so very wide,
You needs must think—if you should think—
   The lily maid had died.

Save that, a little way away,
    I'd watch you for a little while,
To see you speak, the way you speak,
    And smile,—if you should smile.

BURIAL

MINE is a body that should die at sea!
  And have for a grave, instead of a grave
Six feet deep and the length of me,
  All the water that is under the wave!

And terrible fishes to seize my flesh,
  Such as a living man might fear,
And eat me while I am firm and fresh,—
  Not wait till I've been dead for a year!

MARIPOSA

BUTTERFLIES are white and blue
In this field we wander through.
Suffer me to take your hand.
Death comes in a day or two.

All the things we ever knew
Will be ashes in that hour,
Mark the transient butterfly,
How he hangs upon the flower.

Suffer me to take your hand.
Suffer me to cherish you
Till the dawn is in the sky.
Whether I be false or true,
Death comes in a day or two.

THE LITTLE HILL

Oh, here the air is sweet and still,
　　And soft's the grass to lie on;
And far away's the little hill
　　They took for Christ to die on.

And there's a hill across the brook,
　　And down the brook's another;
But, oh, the little hill they took,—
　　I think I am its mother!

The moon that saw Gethsemane,
　　I watch it rise and set;
It has so many things to see,
　　They help it to forget.

But little hills that sit at home
　　So many hundred years,
Remember Greece, remember Rome,
　　Remember Mary's tears.

And far away in Palestine,
    Sadder than any other,
Grieves still the hill that I call mine,—
    I think I am its mother!

DOUBT NO MORE THAT OBERON

Doubt no more that Oberon—
Never doubt that Pan
Lived, and played a reed, and ran
After nymphs in a dark forest,
In the merry, credulous days,—
Lived, and led a fairy band
Over the indulgent land!
Ah, for in this dourest, sorest
Age man's eye has looked upon,
Death to fauns and death to fays,
Still the dog-wood dares to raise—
Healthy tree, with trunk and root—
Ivory bowls that bear no fruit,
And the starlings and the jays—
Birds that cannot even sing—
Dare to come again in spring!

LAMENT

Listen, children:
Your father is dead.
From his old coats
I'll make you little jackets;
I'll make you little trousers
From his old pants.
There'll be in his pockets
Things he used to put there,
Keys and pennies
Covered with tobacco;
Dan shall have the pennies
To save in his bank;
Anne shall have the keys
To make a pretty noise with.
Life must go on,
And the dead be forgotten;
Life must go on,
Though good men die;
Anne, eat your breakfast;
Dan, take your medicine;
Life must go on;
I forget just why.

EXILED

Searching my heart for its true sorrow,
  This is the thing I find to be:
That I am weary of words and people,
  Sick of the city, wanting the sea;

Wanting the sticky, salty sweetness
  Of the strong wind and shattered spray;
Wanting the loud sound and the soft sound
  Of the big surf that breaks all day.

Always before about my dooryard,
  Marking the reach of the winter sea,
Rooted in sand and dragging drift-wood,
  Straggled the purple wild sweet-pea;

Always I climbed the wave at morning,
  Shook the sand from my shoes at night,
That now am caught beneath great buildings,
  Stricken with noise, confused with light.

If I could hear the green piles groaning
  Under the windy wooden piers,

See once again the bobbing barrels,
    And the black sticks that fence the weirs,

If I could see the weedy mussels
    Crusting the wrecked and rotting hulls,
Hear once again the hungry crying
    Overhead, of the wheeling gulls,

Feel once again the shanty straining
    Under the turning of the tide,
Fear once again the rising freshet,
    Dread the bell in the fog outside,—

I should be happy,—that was happy
    All day long on the coast of Maine!
I have a need to hold and handle
    Shells and anchors and ships again!

I should be happy, that am happy
    Never at all since I came here.
I am too long away from water.
    I have a need of water near.

THE DEATH OF AUTUMN

WHEN reeds are dead and a straw to thatch the
marshes,
And feathered pampas-grass rides into the wind
Like aged warriors westward, tragic, thinned
Of half their tribe, and over the flattened rushes,
Stripped of its secret, open, stark and bleak,
Blackens afar the half-forgotten creek,—
Then leans on me the weight of the year, and
crushes
My heart. I know that Beauty must ail and die,
And will be born again,—but ah, to see
Beauty stiffened, staring up at the sky!
Oh, Autumn! Autumn!—What is the Spring to
me?

ODE TO SILENCE

Aye, but she?
Your other sister and my other soul
Grave Silence, lovelier
Than the three loveliest maidens, what of her?
Clio, not you,
Not you, Calliope,
Nor all your wanton line,
Not Beauty's perfect self shall comfort me
For Silence once departed,
For her the cool-tongued, her the tranquil-
    hearted,
Whom evermore I follow wistfully,
Wandering Heaven and Earth and Hell and the
    four seasons through;
Thalia, not you,
Not you, Melpomene,
Not your incomparable feet, O thin Terpsichore,
I seek in this great hall,
But one more pale, more pensive, most beloved of
    you all.

I seek her from afar.

I come from temples where her altars are,

From groves that bear her name,

Noisy with stricken victims now and sacrificial
flame,

And cymbals struck on high and strident faces

Obstreperous in her praise

They neither love nor know,

A goddess of gone days,

Departed long ago,

Abandoning the invaded shrines and fanes

Of her old sanctuary,

A deity obscure and legendary,

Of whom there now remains,

For sages to decipher and priests to garble,

Only and for a little while her letters wedged in
marble,

Which even now, behold, the friendly mumbling
rain erases,

And the inarticulate snow,

Leaving at last of her least signs and traces

None whatsoever, nor whither she is vanished from
these places.

"She will love well," I said,
"If love be of that heart inhabiter,
The flowers of the dead;
The red anemone that with no sound
Moves in the wind, and from another wound
That sprang, the heavily-sweet blue hyacinth,
That blossoms underground,
And sallow poppies, will be dear to her.
And will not Silence know
In the black shade of what obsidian steep
Stiffens the white narcissus numb with sleep?
(Seed which Demeter's daughter bore from home,
Uptorn by desperate fingers long ago,
Reluctant even as she,
Undone Persephone,
And even as she set out again to grow
In twilight, in perdition's lean and inauspicious
    loam).
She will love well," I said,
"The flowers of the dead;
Where dark Persephone the winter round,
Uncomforted for home, uncomforted,
Lacking a sunny southern slope in northern Sicily,

With sullen pupils focussed on a dream,
Stares on the stagnant stream
That moats the unequivocable battlements of
    Hell,
There, there will she be found,
She that is Beauty veiled from men and Music in
    a swound."

"I long for Silence as they long for breath
Whose helpless nostrils drink the bitter sea;
What thing can be
So stout, what so redoubtable, in Death
What fury, what considerable rage, if only she,
Upon whose icy breast,
Unquestioned, uncaressed,
One time I lay,
And whom always I lack,
Even to this day,
Being by no means from that frigid bosom weaned
    away,
If only she therewith be given me back?"

I sought her down that dolorous labyrinth,

Wherein no shaft of sunlight ever fell,

And in among the bloodless everywhere

I sought her, but the air,

Breathed many times and spent,

Was fretful with a whispering discontent,

And questioning me, importuning me to tell

Some slightest tidings of the light of day they know
no more.

Plucking my sleeve, the eager shades were with me
where I went.

I paused at every grievous door,

And harked a moment, holding up my hand,—
and for a space

A hush was on them, while they watched my
face;

And then they fell a-whispering as before;

So that I smiled at them and left them, seeing she
was not there.

I sought her, too,

Among the upper gods, although I knew

She was not like to be where feasting is,

Nor near to Heaven's lord,

Being a thing abhorred
And shunned of him, although a child of his,
(Not yours, not yours; to you she owes not
 breath,
Mother of Song, being sown of Zeus upon a dream
 of Death).
Fearing to pass unvisited some place
And later learn, too late, how all the while,
With her still face,
She had been standing there and seen me pass, with-
 out a smile,
I sought her even to the sagging board whereat
The stout immortals sat;
But such a laughter shook the mighty hall
No one could hear me say:
Had she been seen upon the Hill that day?
And no one knew at all
How long I stood, or when at last I sighed and
 went away.

There is a garden lying in a lull
Between the mountains and the mountainous sea,
I know not where, but which a dream diurnal

Paints on my lids a moment till the hull
Be lifted from the kernel
And Slumber fed to me.
Your foot-print is not there, Mnemosene,
Though it would seem a ruined place and after
Your lichenous heart, being full
Of broken columns, caryatides
Thrown to the earth and fallen forward on their
    jointless knees,
And urns funereal altered into dust
Minuter than the ashes of the dead,
And Psyche's lamp out of the earth up-thrust,
Dripping itself in marble wax on what was once
    the bed
Of Love, and his young body asleep, but now is
    dust instead.

There twists the bitter-sweet, the white wisteria
Fastens its fingers in the strangling wall,
And the wide crannies quicken with bright weeds;
There dumbly like a worm all day the still white
    orchid feeds;
But never an echo of your daughters' laughter

Is there, nor any sign of you at all
Swells fungous from the rotten bough, grey mother
    of Pieria!

Only her shadow once upon a stone
I saw,—and, lo, the shadow and the garden, too,
    were gone.

I tell you you have done her body an ill,
You chatterers, you noisy crew!
She is not anywhere!
I sought her in deep Hell;
And through the world as well;
I thought of Heaven and I sought her there;
Above nor under ground
Is Silence to be found,
That was the very warp and woof of you,
Lovely before your songs began and after they were
    through!
Oh, say if on this hill
Somewhere your sister's body lies in death,
So I may follow there, and make a wreath

Of my locked hands, that on her quiet breast
Shall lie till age has withered them!

                    (Ah, sweetly from the rest
I see
Turn and consider me
Compassionate Euterpe!)
"There is a gate beyond the gate of Death,
Beyond the gate of everlasting Life,
Beyond the gates of Heaven and Hell," she saith,
"Whereon but to believe is horror!
Whereon to meditate engendereth
Even in deathless spirits such as I
A tumult in the breath,
A chilling of the inexhaustible blood
Even in my veins that never will be dry,
And in the austere, divine monotony
That is my being, the madness of an unaccustomed
      mood.

This is her province whom you lack and seek;
And seek her not elsewhere.
Hell is a thoroughfare

For pilgrims,—Herakles,

And he that loved Euridice too well,

Have walked therein; and many more than these;

And witnessed the desire and the despair

Of souls that passed reluctantly and sicken for the
air;

You, too, have entered Hell,

And issued thence; but thence whereof I speak

None has returned;—for thither fury brings

Only the driven ghosts of them that flee before all
things.

Oblivion is the name of this abode: and she is
there."

Oh, radiant Song! Oh, gracious Memory!

Be long upon this height

I shall not climb again!

I know the way you mean,—the little night,

And the long empty day,—never to see

Again the angry light,

Or hear the hungry noises cry my brain!

Ah, but she,
Your other sister and my other soul,
She shall again be mine;
And I shall drink her from a silver bowl,
A chilly thin green wine,
Not bitter to the taste,
Not sweet,
Not of your press, oh, restless, clamorous nine,—
To foam beneath the frantic hoofs of mirth—
But savoring faintly of the acid earth,
And trod by pensive feet
From perfect clusters ripened without haste
Out of the urgent heat
In some clear glimmering vaulted twilight under
    the odorous vine.

Lift up your lyres! Sing on!
But as for me, I seek your sister whither she is
    gone.

MEMORIAL TO D. C.
[VASSAR COLLEGE, 1918]

Oh, loveliest throat of all sweet throats,
  Where now no more the music is,
With hands that wrote you little notes
  I write you little elegies!

EPITAPH

HEAP not on this mound
   Roses that she loved so well;
Why bewilder her with roses,
   That she cannot see or smell?
She is happy where she lies
   With the dust upon her eyes.

PRAYER TO PERSEPHONE

BE to her, Persephone,
All the things I might not be;
Take her head upon your knee.
She that was so proud and wild,
Flippant, arrogant and free,
She that had no need of me,
Is a little lonely child
Lost in Hell,—Persephone,
Take her head upon your knee;
Say to her, "My dear, my dear,
It is not so dreadful here."

CHORUS

GIVE away her gowns,
Give away her shoes;
She has no more use
For her fragrant gowns;
Take them all down,
Blue, green, blue,
Lilac, pink, blue,
From their padded hangers;
She will dance no more
In her narrow shoes;
Sweep her narrow shoes
From the closet floor.

ELEGY

Let them bury your big eyes
In the secret earth securely,
Your thin fingers, and your fair,
Soft, indefinite-colored hair,—
All of these in some way, surely,
From the secret earth shall rise;
Not for these I sit and stare,
Broken and bereft completely;
Your young flesh that sat so neatly
On your little bones will sweetly
Blossom in the air.

But your voice,—never the rushing
Of a river underground,
Not the rising of the wind
In the trees before the rain,
Not the woodcock's watery call,
Not the note the white-throat utters,
Not the feet of children pushing
Yellow leaves along the gutters
In the blue and bitter fall,

Shall content my musing mind
For the beauty of that sound
That in no new way at all
Ever will be heard again.

Sweetly through the sappy stalk
Of the vigorous weed,
Holding all it held before,
Cherished by the faithful sun,
On and on eternally
Shall your altered fluid run,
Bud and bloom and go to seed;
But your singing days are done;
But the music of your talk
Never shall the chemistry
Of the secret earth restore.
All your lovely words are spoken.
Once the ivory box is broken,
Beats the golden bird no more.

DIRGE

Boys and girls that held her dear,
  Do your weeping now;
All you loved of her lies here.

Brought to earth the arrogant brow,
  And the withering tongue
Chastened; do your weeping now.

Sing whatever songs are sung,
  Wind whatever wreath,
For a playmate perished young,

For a spirit spent in death.
Boys and girls that held her dear,
All you loved of her lies here.

SONNETS

WE talk of taxes, and I call you friend;
Well, such you are,—but well enough we know
How thick about us root, how rankly grow
Those subtle weeds no man has need to tend,
That flourish through neglect, and soon must send
Perfume too sweet upon us and overthrow
Our steady senses; how such matters go
We are aware, and how such matters end.
Yet shall be told no meagre passion here;
With lovers such as we forevermore
Isolde drinks the draught, and Guinevere
Receives the Table's ruin through her door,
Francesca, with the loud surf at her ear,
Lets fall the colored book upon the floor.

Into the golden vessel of great song
Let us pour all our passion; breast to breast
Let other lovers lie, in love and rest;
Not we,—articulate, so, but with the tongue
Of all the world: the churning blood, the long
Shuddering quiet, the desperate hot palms pressed
Sharply together upon the escaping guest,
The common soul, unguarded, and grown strong.
Longing alone is singer to the lute;
Let still on nettles in the open sigh
The minstrel, that in slumber is as mute
As any man, and love be far and high,
That else forsakes the topmost branch, a fruit
Found on the ground by every passer-by.

III

Not with libations, but with shouts and laughter
We drenched the altars of Love's sacred grove,
Shaking to earth green fruits, impatient after
The launching of the colored moths of Love.
Love's proper myrtle and his mother's zone
We bound about our irreligious brows,
And fettered him with garlands of our own,
And spread a banquet in his frugal house.
Not yet the god has spoken; but I fear
Though we should break our bodies in his flame,
And pour our blood upon his altar, here
Henceforward is a grove without a name,
A pasture to the shaggy goats of Pan,
Whence flee forever a woman and a man.

Only until this cigarette is ended,
A little moment at the end of all,
While on the floor the quiet ashes fall,
And in the firelight to a lance extended,
Bizarrely with the jazzing music blended,
The broken shadow dances on the wall,
I will permit my memory to recall
The vision of you, by all my dreams attended.
And then adieu,—farewell!—the dream is done.
Yours is a face of which I can forget
The color and the features, every one,
The words not ever, and the smiles not yet;
But in your day this moment is the sun
Upon a hill, after the sun has set.

V

Once more into my arid days like dew,
Like wind from an oasis, or the sound
Of cold sweet water bubbling underground,
A treacherous messenger, the thought of you
Comes to destroy me; once more I renew
Firm faith in your abundance, whom I found
Long since to be but just one other mound
Of sand, whereon no green thing ever grew.
And once again, and wiser in no wise,
I chase your colored phantom on the air,
And sob and curse and fall and weep and rise
And stumble pitifully on to where,
Miserable and lost, with stinging eyes,
Once more I clasp,—and there is nothing there.

No rose that in a garden ever grew,
In Homer's or in Omar's or in mine,
Though buried under centuries of fine
Dead dust of roses, shut from sun and dew
Forever, and forever lost from view,
But must again in fragrance rich as wine
The grey aisles of the air incarnadine
When the old summers surge into a new.
Thus when I swear, "I love with all my heart,"
'Tis with the heart of Lilith that I swear,
'Tis with the love of Lesbia and Lucrece;
And thus as well my love must lose some part
Of what it is, had Helen been less fair,
Or perished young, or stayed at home in Greece.

When I too long have looked upon your face,
Wherein for me a brightness unobscured
Save by the mists of brightness has its place,
And terrible beauty not to be endured,
I turn away reluctant from your light,
And stand irresolute, a mind undone,
A silly, dazzled thing deprived of sight
From having looked too long upon the sun.
Then is my daily life a narrow room
In which a little while, uncertainly,
Surrounded by impenetrable gloom,
Among familiar things grown strange to me
Making my way, I pause, and feel, and hark,
Till I become accustomed to the dark.

And you as well must die, belovèd dust,
And all your beauty stand you in no stead;
This flawless, vital hand, this perfect head,
This body of flame and steel, before the gust
Of Death, or under his autumnal frost,
Shall be as any leaf, be no less dead
Than the first leaf that fell,—this wonder fled.
Altered, estranged, disintegrated, lost.
Nor shall my love avail you in your hour.
In spite of all my love, you will arise
Upon that day and wander down the air
Obscurely as the unattended flower,
It mattering not how beautiful you were,
Or how belovèd above all else that dies.

Let you not say of me when I am old,
In pretty worship of my withered hands
Forgetting who I am, and how the sands
Of such a life as mine run red and gold
Even to the ultimate sifting dust, "Behold,
Here walketh passionless age!"—for there expands
A curious superstition in these lands,
And by its leave some weightless tales are told.

In me no lenten wicks watch out the night;
I am the booth where Folly holds her fair;
Impious no less in ruin than in strength,
When I lie crumbled to the earth at length,
Let you not say, "Upon this reverend site
The righteous groaned and beat their breasts in
     prayer."

Oh, my belovèd, have you thought of this:
How in the years to come unscrupulous Time,
More cruel than Death, will tear you from my kiss,
And make you old, and leave me in my prime?
How you and I, who scale together yet
A little while the sweet, immortal height
No pilgrim may remember or forget,
As sure as the world turns, some granite night
Shall lie awake and know the gracious flame
Gone out forever on the mutual stone;
And call to mind that on the day you came
I was a child, and you a hero grown?—
And the night pass, and the strange morning break
Upon our anguish for each other's sake!

As to some lovely temple, tenantless
Long since, that once was sweet with shivering
    brass,
Knowing well its altars ruined and the grass
Grown up between the stones, yet from excess
Of grief hard driven, or great loneliness,
The worshiper returns, and those who pass
Marvel him crying on a name that was,—
So is it now with me in my distress.
Your body was a temple to Delight;
Cold are its ashes whence the breath is fled,
Yet here one time your spirit was wont to move;
Here might I hope to find you day or night,
And here I come to look for you, my love,
Even now, foolishly, knowing you are dead.

Cherish you then the hope I shall forget
At length, my lord, Pieria?—put away
For your so passing sake, this mouth of clay
These mortal bones against my body set,
For all the puny fever and frail sweat
Of human love,—renounce for these, I say,
The Singing Mountain's memory, and betray
The silent lyre that hangs upon me yet?
Ah, but indeed, some day shall you awake,
Rather, from dreams of me, that at your side
So many nights, a lover and a bride,
But stern in my soul's chastity, have lain,
To walk the world forever for my sake,
And in each chamber find me gone again!

WILD SWANS

*I looked in my heart while the wild swans went
over.*
And what did I see I had not seen before?
Only a question less or a question more;
Nothing to match the flight of wild birds flying.
Tiresome heart, forever living and dying,
House without air, I leave you and lock your door.
Wild swans, come over the town, come over
The town again, trailing your legs and crying!

THE BUCK IN THE SNOW
AND OTHER POEMS

CONTENTS

PART ONE

PART TWO

PART THREE

Part Four

PART ONE

MORITURUS

If I could have
  Two things in one:
The peace of the grave,
  And the light of the sun:

My hands across
  My thin breast-bone,
But aware of the moss
  Invading the stone,

Aware of the flight
  Of the golden flicker
With his wing to the light;
  To hear him nicker

And drum with his bill
  On the rotted willow;
Snug and still
  On a grey pillow

Deep in the clay
  Where digging is hard,
Out of the way,—
  The blue shard

Of a broken platter—
    If I might be
Insensate matter
    With sensate me

Sitting within,
    Harking and prying,
I might begin
    To dicker with dying.

For the body at best
    Is a bundle of aches,
Longing for rest;
    It cries when it wakes

"Alas, 'tis light!"
    At set of sun
"Alas, 'tis night,
    And nothing done!"

Death, however,
    Is a spongy wall,
Is a sticky river,
    Is nothing at all.

Summon the weeper,
　　Wail and sing;
Call him Reaper,
　　Angel, King;

Call him Evil
　　Drunk to the lees,
Monster, Devil,—
　　He is less than these.

Call him Thief,
　　The Maggot in the Cheese,
The Canker in the Leaf,—
　　He is less than these.

Dusk without sound,
　　Where the spirit by pain
Uncoiled, is wound
　　To spring again;

The mind enmeshed
　　Laid straight in repose,
And the body refreshed
　　By feeding the rose,—

These are but visions;
　　These would be

The grave's derisions,
  Could the grave see.

Here is the wish
  Of one that died
Like a beached fish
  On the ebb of the tide:

That he might wait
  Till the tide came back,
To see if a crate,
  Or a bottle, or a black

Boot, or an oar
  Or an orange peel
Be washed ashore. . . .
  About his heel

The sand slips;
  The last he hears
From the world's lips
  Is the sand in his ears.

What thing is little?—
  The aphis hid
In a house of spittle?
  The hinge of the lid

Of the spider's eye
　　At the spider's birth?
"Greater am I
　　By the earth's girth

"Than Mighty Death!"
　　All creatures cry
That can summon breath;—
　　And speak no lie.

For He is nothing;
　　He is less
Than Echo answering
　　"Nothingness!"—

Less than the heat
　　Of the furthest star
To the ripening wheat;
　　Less by far,

When all the lipping
　　Is said and sung,
Than the sweat dripping
　　From a dog's tongue.

This being so,
　　And I being such,

I would liever go
  On a cripple's crutch,

Lopped and felled;
  Liever be dependent
On a chair propelled
  By a surly attendant

With a foul breath,
  And be spooned my food,
Than go with Death
  Where nothing good,

Not even the thrust
  Of the summer gnat,
Consoles the dust
  For being that.

Needy, lonely,
  Stitched by pain,
Left with only
  The drip of the rain

Out of all I had;
  The books of the wise,
Badly read
  By other eyes,

Lewdly bawled
  At my closing ear;
Hated, called
  A lingerer here;—

Withstanding Death
  Till Life be gone,
I shall treasure my breath,
  I shall linger on.

I shall bolt my door
  With a bolt and a cable;
I shall block my door
  With a bureau and a table;

With all my might
  My door shall be barred.
I shall put up a fight,
  I shall take it hard.

With his hand on my mouth
  He shall drag me forth,
Shrieking to the south
  And clutching at the north.

SONG

GONE, gone again is Summer the lovely.
　　She that knew not where to hide,
Is gone again like a jeweled fish from the hand,
　　Is lost on every side.

Mute, mute, I make my way to the garden,
　　Thither where she last was seen;
The heavy foot of the frost is on the flags there,
　　Where her light step has been.

Gone, gone again is Summer the lovely,
　　Gone again on every side,
Lost again like a shining fish from the hand
　　Into the shadowy tide.

TO THE WIFE OF A SICK FRIEND

SHELTER this candle from the wind.
Hold it steady. In its light
The cave wherein we wander lost
Glitters with frosty stalactite,
Blossoms with mineral rose and lotus,
Sparkles with crystal moon and star,
Till a man would rather be lost than found:
We have forgotten where we are.

Shelter this candle. Shrewdly blowing
Down the cave from a secret door
Enters our only foe, the wind.
Hold it steady. Lest we stand,
Each in a sudden, separate dark,
The hot wax spattered upon your hand,
The smoking wick in my nostrils strong,
The inner eyelid red and green
For a moment yet with moons and roses,—
Then the unmitigated dark.

Alone, alone, in a terrible place,
In utter dark without a face,
With only the dripping of the water on the stone,
And the sound of your tears, and the taste of my
        own.

THE BOBOLINK

BLACK bird scudding
Under the rainy sky,
How wet your wings must be!
And your small head how sleek and cold with
water.

Oh, Bobolink, 'tis you!
Over the buffeted orchard in the summer draught,
Chuckling and singing, charging the rainy cloud,
A little bird gone daft,
A little bird with a secret.

Only the bobolink on the rainy
Rhubarb blossom,
Knows my heart.
For whom adversity has not a word to say that
can be heard
Above the din of summer.
The rain has taught us nothing. And the hooves of
cattle, and the cat in the grass
Have taught us nothing.
The hawk that motionless above the hill
In the pure sky
Stands like a blackened planet
Has taught us nothing,—seeing him shut his wings
and fall

Has taught us nothing at all.
In the shadow of the hawk we feather our nests.

Bobolink, you and I, an airy fool and an earthy,
Chuckling under the rain!

I shall never be sad again.
I shall never be sad again.

Ah, sweet, absurd,
Belovèd, bedraggled bird!

THE HAWKWEED

BETWEEN the red-top and the rye,
  Between the buckwheat and the corn,
The ploughman sees with sullen eye
The hawkweed licking at the sky:

  Three level acres all forlorn,
  Unfertile, sour, outrun, outworn,
  Free as the day that they were born.

Southward and northward, west and east,
  The sulphate and the lime are spread;
Harrowed and sweetened, urged, increased,
The furrow sprouts for man and beast:

  While of the hawkweed's radiant head
  No stanchion reeks, no stock is fed.

Triumphant up the taken field
  The tractor and the plough advance;
Blest be the healthy germ concealed
In the rich earth, and blest the yield:

  And blest be Beauty, that enchants
  The frail, the solitary lance.

TO A FRIEND ESTRANGED FROM ME

Now goes under, and I watch it go under, the sun
That will not rise again.
Today has seen the setting, in your eyes cold and
senseless as the sea,
Of friendship better than bread, and of bright
charity
That lifts a man a little above the beasts that run.

That this could be!
That I should live to see
Most vulgar Pride, that stale obstreperous clown,
So fitted out with purple robe and crown
To stand among his betters! Face to face
With outraged me in this once holy place,
Where Wisdom was a favoured guest and hunted
Truth was harboured out of danger,
He bulks enthroned, a lewd, an insupportable
stranger!

I would have sworn, indeed I swore it:
The hills may shift, the waters may decline,
Winter may twist the stem from the twig that
bore it,
But never your love from me, your hand from
mine.

Now goes under the sun, and I watch it go under.
Farewell, sweet light, great wonder!
You, too, farewell,—but fare not well enough to
dream
You have done wisely to invite the night before
the darkness came.

THE ROAD TO AVRILLE

APRIL again in Avrillé,
  And the brown lark in air.
And you and I a world apart,
  That walked together there.

The cuckoo spoke from out the wood,
  The lark from out the sky.
Embraced upon the highway stood
  Love-sick you and I.

The rosy peasant left his bees,
  The carrier slowed his cart,
To shout us blithe obscenities,
  And bless us from the heart,

That long before the year was out,
  Under the autumn rain,
Far from the road to Avrillé,
  Parted with little pain.

FOR PAO-CHIN,
A BOATMAN ON THE YELLOW SEA

WHERE is he now, in his soiled shirt reeking of
    garlic,
Sculling his sampan home, and night approaching
    fast—
The red sail hanging wrinkled on the bamboo mast;

Where is he now, I shall remember my whole life
    long
With love and praise, for the sake of a small song
Played on a Chinese flute?
                    I have been sad;
I have been in cities where the song was all I had,—
A treasure never to be bartered by the hungry days.

Where is he now, for whom I carry in my heart
This love, this praise?

NORTHERN APRIL

O MIND, beset by music never for a moment quiet,—
The wind at the flue, the wind strumming the
    shutter;
The soft, antiphonal speech of the doubled brook,
    never for a moment quiet;
The rush of the rain against the glass, his voice in
    the eaves-gutter!

Where shall I lay you to sleep, and the robins be
    quiet?
Lay you to sleep—and the frogs be silent in the
    marsh?
Crashes the sleet from the bough and the bough
    sighs upward, never for a moment quiet.
April is upon us, pitiless and young and harsh.

O April, full of blood, full of breath, have pity upon
    us!
Pale, where the winter like a stone has been lifted
    away, we emerge like yellow grass.
Be for a moment quiet, buffet us not, have pity
    upon us,
Till the green come back into the vein, till the
    giddiness pass.

THERE AT DUSK I FOUND YOU

THERE at dusk I found you, walking and weeping
Upon the broken flags,
Where at dusk the dumb white nicotine awakes and
    utters her fragrance
In a garden sleeping.

Looking askance you said:
Love is dead.

Under our eyes without warning softly the summer
    afternoon let fall
The rose upon the wall,
And it lay there spintered.
Terribly then into my heart the forgotten anguish
    entered.

I saw the dark stone on the smallest finger of
    your hand,
And the clean cuff above.
No more, no more the dark stone on the smallest
    finger
Of your brown and naked arm,
Lifting my body in love!

Worse than dead is he of the wounded wing,
Who walks between us, weeping upon the cold
flags,
Bleeding and weeping, dragging his broken wing.
He has gathered the rose into his hand and chafed
her with his breath.
But the rose is quiet and pale. She has forgotten
us all.
Even spring.
Even death.

As for me, I have forgotten nothing,—nor shall I
ever forget—
But this one thing:
I have forgotten which of us it was
That hurt his wing.
I only know his limping flight above us in the blue
air
Toward the sunset cloud
Is more than I can bear.

You, you there,
Stiff-necked and angry, holding up your head so
proud,
Have you not seen how pitiful lame he flies, and
none to befriend him?
Speak! Are you blind? Are you dead?
Shall we call him back? Shall we mend him?

BEING YOUNG AND GREEN

BEING young and green, I said in love's despite:
Never in the world will I to living wight
Give over, air my mind
To anyone,
Hang out its ancient secrets in the strong wind
To be shredded and faded. . . .

Oh, me, invaded
And sacked by the wind and the sun!

MIST IN THE VALLEY

THESE hills, to hurt me more,
That am hurt already enough,—
Having left the sea behind,
Having turned suddenly and left the shore
That I had loved beyond all words, even a song's
    words, to convey,

And built me a house on upland acres,
Sweet with the pinxter, bright and rough
With the rusty blackbird long before the winter's
    done,
But smelling never of bayberry hot in the sun,
Nor ever loud with the pounding of the long white
    breakers,—

These hills, beneath the October moon,
Sit in the valley white with mist
Like islands in a quiet bay,

Jut out from shore into the mist,
Wooded with poplar dark as pine,
Like points of land into a quiet bay.

(Just in that way
The harbour met the bay)

23

Stricken too sore for tears,
I stand, remembering the islands and the sea's lost
    sound. . . .
Life at its best no longer than the sand-peep's cry,
And I two years, two years,
Tilling an upland ground!

THE HARDY GARDEN

Now LET forever the phlox and the rose be tended
Here where the rain has darkened and the sun has
   dried
So many times the terrace, yet is love unended,
  Love has not died.

Let here no seed of a season, that the winter
But once assails, take root and for a time endure;
But only such as harbour at the frozen centre
  The germ secure.

Set here the phlox and the iris, and establish
Pink and valerian, and the great and lesser bells;
But suffer not the sisters of the year, to publish
  That frost prevails.

How far from home in a world of mortal burdens
Is Love, that may not die, and is forever young!
Set roses here: surround her only with such maidens
  As speak her tongue.

THE PIGEONS

WELL I remember the pigeons in the sunny arbor
Beyond your open door;
How they conversed throughout the afternoon in
their monotonous voices never for a moment
still;
Always of yesterday they spoke, and of the days
before,
Rustling the vine-leaves, twitching the dark shadows of the leaves on the bright sill.

You said, the soft curring and droning of the
pigeons in the vine
Was a pretty thing enough to the passer-by,
But a maddening thing to the man with his head
in his hands,—"Like mine! Like mine!"
You said, and ran to the door and waved them off
into the sky.

They did not come back. The arbor was empty of
their cooing.
The shadows of the leaves were still. "Whither
have they flown, then?"
I said, and waited for their wings, but they did not
come back. If I had known then
What I know now, I never would have left your
door.

Tall in your faded smock, with steady hand
Mingling the brilliant pigments, painting your
   intersecting planes you stand,
In a quiet room, empty of the past, of its droning
   and cooing,
Thinking I know not what, but thinking of me no
   more,
That left you with a light word, that loving and
   rueing
Walk in the streets of a city you have never seen,
Walk in a noise of yesterday and of the days
   before,
Walk in a cloud of wings intolerable, shutting out
   the sun as if it never had been.

THE BUCK IN THE SNOW

WHITE sky, over the hemlocks bowed with snow,
Saw you not at the beginning of evening the antlered
    buck and his doe
Standing in the apple-orchard? I saw them. I saw
    them suddenly go,
Tails up, with long leaps lovely and slow,
Over the stone-wall into the wood of hemlocks
    bowed with snow.

Now lies he here, his wild blood scalding the snow.

How strange a thing is death, bringing to his knees,
    bringing to his antlers
The buck in the snow.
How strange a thing,—a mile away by now, it may
    be,
Under the heavy hemlocks that as the moments
    pass
Shift their loads a little, letting fall a feather of
    snow—
Life, looking out attentive from the eyes of the doe.

PART TWO

PART TWO

THE ANGUISH

I WOULD to God I were quenched and fed
As in my youth
From the flask of song, and the good bread
Of beauty richer than truth.

The anguish of the world is on my tongue.
My bowl is filled to the brim with it; there is more
    than I can eat.
Happy are the toothless old and the toothless
    young,
That cannot rend this meat.

JUSTICE DENIED IN MASSACHUSETTS

Let us abandon then our gardens and go home
And sit in the sitting-room.
Shall the larkspur blossom or the corn grow under
    this cloud?
Sour to the fruitful seed
Is the cold earth under this cloud,
Fostering quack and weed, we have marched upon
    but cannot conquer;
We have bent the blades of our hoes against the
    stalks of them.

Let us go home, and sit in the sitting-room.
Not in our day
Shall the cloud go over and the sun rise as before,
Beneficent upon us
Out of the glittering bay,
And the warm winds be blown inward from the sea
Moving the blades of corn
With a peaceful sound.
Forlorn, forlorn,
Stands the blue hay-rack by the empty mow.
And the petals drop to the ground,
Leaving the tree unfruited.
The sun that warmed our stooping backs and with-
    ered the weed uprooted—

We shall not feel it again.
We shall die in darkness, and be buried in the rain.

What from the splendid dead
We have inherited—
Furrows sweet to the grain, and the weed subdued—
See now the slug and the mildew plunder.
Evil does overwhelm
The larkspur and the corn;
We have seen them go under.

Let us sit here, sit still,
Here in the sitting-room until we die;
At the step of Death on the walk, rise and go;
Leaving to our children's children this beautiful
    doorway,
And this elm,
And a blighted earth to till
With a broken hoe.

HANGMAN'S OAK

BEFORE the cock in the barnyard spoke,
 Before it well was day,
Horror like a serpent from about the Hangman's
 Oak
 Uncoiled and slid away.

Pity and Peace were on the limb
 That bore such bitter fruit.
Deep he lies, and the desperate blood of him
 Befriends the innocent root.

Brother, I said to the air beneath the bough
 Whence he had swung,
It will not be long for any of us now;
 We do not grow young.

It will not be long for the knotter of ropes, not long
 For the sheriff or for me,
Or for any of them that came five hundred strong
 To see you swing from a tree.

Side by side together in the belly of Death
 We sit without hope,
You, and I, and the mother that gave you breath,
 And the tree, and the rope.

WINE FROM THESE GRAPES

WINE from these grapes I shall be treading surely
Morning and noon and night until I die.
Stained with these grapes I shall lie down to die.

If you would speak with me on any matter,
At any time, come where these grapes are grown;
And you will find me treading them to must.
Lean then above me sagely, lest I spatter
Drops of the wine I tread from grapes and dust.

Stained with these grapes I shall lie down to die.
Three women come to wash me clean
Shall not erase this stain.
Nor leave me lying purely,
Awaiting the black lover.
Death, fumbling to uncover
My body in his bed,
Shall know
There has been one
Before him.

TO THOSE WITHOUT PITY

CRUEL of heart, lay down my song.
Your reading eyes have done me wrong.
Not for you was the pen bitten,
And the mind wrung, and the song written.

PART THREE

DAWN

ALL men are lonely now.
This is the hour when no man has a friend.
Memory and Faith suspend
From their spread wings above a cool abyss.
All friendships end.

He that lay awake
All night
For sweet love's unregenerate sake,
Sleeps in the grey light.

The lover, if he dream at all,
Dreams not of her whose languid hand sleeps open
    at his side;
He is gone to another bride.
And she he leaves behind
Sighs not in sleep "Unkind . . . unkind . . .";
She walks in a garden of yellow quinces;
Smiling, she gathers yellow quinces in a basket
Of willow and laurel combined.

Should I return to your door,
Fresh and haggard out of the morning air,
There would be darkness on the stair,
And a dead close odor painfully sad,

That was not there before.
There would be silence. There would be heavy
    steps across the floor.
And you would let me in, frowning with sleep
Under your rumpled hair.

Beautiful now upon the ear unshut by slumber
The rich and varied voices of the waking day!—
The mighty, mournful whistles without number
Of tugs and ferries, mingling, confounding, failing,
Thinning to separate notes of wailing,
Making stupendous music on the misty bay.

Now through the echoing street in the growing light,
Intent on errands that the sun approves,
Clatter unashamed the heavy wheels and hooves
Before the silent houses; briskly they say:
"Marshal not me among the enterprises of the
    night.
I am the beginning of the day."

TO A YOUNG GIRL

SHALL I despise you that your colourless tears
Made rainbows in your lashes, and you forgot to
  weep?
Would we were half so wise, that eke a grief out
By sitting in the dark, until we fall asleep.

I only fear lest, being by nature sunny,
By and by you will weep no more at all,
And fall asleep in the light, having lost with the
  tears
The colour in the lashes that comes as the tears fall.

I would not have you darken your lids with weep-
  ing,
Beautiful eyes, but I would have you weep enough
To wet the fingers of the hand held over the eye-lids,
And stain a little the light frock's delicate stuff.

For there came into my mind, as I watched you
  winking the tears down,
Laughing faces, blown from the west and the east,
Faces lovely and proud that I have prized and
  cherished;
Nor were the loveliest among them those that had
  wept the least.

EVENING ON LESBOS

Twice having seen your shingled heads adorable
Side by side, the onyx and the gold,
I know that I have had what I could not hold.

Twice have I entered the room, not knowing she
    was here.
Two agate eyes, two eyes of malachite,
Twice have been turned upon me, hard and bright.

Whereby I know my loss.

                          Oh, not restorable
Sweet incense, mounting in the windless night!

DIRGE WITHOUT MUSIC

I AM not resigned to the shutting away of loving
    hearts in the hard ground.
So it is, and so it will be, for so it has been, time
    out of mind:
Into the darkness they go, the wise and the lovely.
    Crowned
With lilies and with laurel they go; but I am not
    resigned.

Lovers and thinkers, into the earth with you.
Be one with the dull, the indiscriminate dust.
A fragment of what you felt, of what you knew,
A formula, a phrase remains,—but the best is lost.

The answers quick and keen, the honest look, the
    laughter, the love,—
They are gone. They are gone to feed the roses.
    Elegant and curled
Is the blossom. Fragrant is the blossom. I know.
    But I do not approve.
More precious was the light in your eyes than all
    the roses of the world.

Down, down, down into the darkness of the grave
Gently they go, the beautiful, the tender, the kind;
Quietly they go, the intelligent, the witty, the brave.
I know. But I do not approve. And I am not
resigned.

MEMORY OF CASSIS

Do you recall how we sat by the smokily-burning
Twisted odorous trunk of the olive-tree,
In the inn on the cliff, and skinned the ripe green
figs,
And heard the white sirocco driving in the sea?

The thunder and the smother there where like a
ship's prow
The light-house breasted the wave? how wanly
through the wild spray
Under our peering eyes the eye of the light looked
out,
Disheveled, but without dismay?

Do you recall the sweet-alyssum over the ledges
Crawling and the tall heather and the mushrooms
under the pines,
And the deep white dust of the broad road leading
outward
To a world forgotten, between the dusty almonds
and the dusty vines?

PORTRAIT

Over and over I have heard,
As now I hear it,
Your voice harsh and light as the scratching of dry
    leaves over the hard ground,
Your voice forever assailed and shaken by the wind
    from the island
Of illustrious living and dead, that never dies down,
And bending at moments under the terrible weight
    of the perfect word,
Here in this room without fire, without comfort of
    any kind,
Reading aloud to me immortal page after page con-
    ceived in a mortal mind.
Beauty at such moments before me like a wild
    bright bird
Has been in the room, and eyed me, and let me
    come near it.

I could not ever nor can I to this day
Acquaint you with the triumph and the sweet rest
These hours have brought to me and always bring,—
Rapture, coloured like the wild bird's neck and
    wing,
Comfort, softer than the feathers of its breast.

Always, and even now, when I rise to go,
Your eyes blaze out from a face gone wickedly pale;
I try to tell you what I would have you know,—
What peace it was; you cry me down; you scourge
    me with a salty flail;
You will not have it so.

WINTER NIGHT

PILE high the hickory and the light
Log of chestnut struck by the blight.
Welcome-in the winter night.

The day has gone in hewing and felling,
Sawing and drawing wood to the dwelling
For the night of talk and story-telling.

These are the hours that give the edge
To the blunted axe and the bent wedge,
Straighten the saw and lighten the sledge.

Here are question and reply,
And the fire reflected in the thinking eye.
So peace, and let the bob-cat cry.

THE CAMEO

FOREVER over now, forever, forever gone
That day. Clear and diminished like a scene
Carven in cameo, the lighthouse, and the cove
    between
The sandy cliffs, and the boat drawn up on the
    beach;
And the long skirt of a lady innocent and young,
Her hand resting on her bosom, her head hung;
And the figure of a man in earnest speech.

Clear and diminished like a scene cut in cameo
The lighthouse, and the boat on the beach, and
    the two shapes
Of the woman and the man; lost like the lost day
Are the words that passed, and the pain,—dis-
    carded, cut away
From the stone, as from the memory the heat of
    the tears escapes.

O troubled forms, O early love unfortunate and
    hard,
Time has estranged you into a jewel cold and pure;
From the action of the waves and from the action
    of sorrow forever secure,
White against a ruddy cliff you stand, chalcedony
    on sard.

COUNTING-OUT RHYME

Silver bark of beech, and sallow
Bark of yellow birch and yellow
   Twig of willow.

Stripe of green in moosewood maple,
Colour seen in leaf of apple,
   Bark of popple.

Wood of popple pale as moonbeam,
Wood of oak for yoke and barn-beam,
   Wood of hornbeam.

Silver bark of beech, and hollow
Stem of elder, tall and yellow
   Twig of willow.

THE PLUM GATHERER

The angry nettle and the mild
  Grew together under the blue-plum trees.
I could not tell as a child
  Which was my friend of these.

Always the angry nettle in the skirt of his sister
  Caught my wrist that reached over the ground,
Where alike I gathered,—for the one was sweet
    and the other wore a frosty dust—
  The broken plum and the sound.

The plum-trees are barren now and the black knot
    is upon them,
  That stood so white in the spring.
I would give, to recall the sweetness and the frost
    of the lost blue plums,
  Anything, anything.
I thrust my arm among the grey ambiguous nettles,
    and wait.
  But they do not sting.

WEST COUNTRY SONG

Sun came up, bigger than all my sorrow;
Lark in air so high, and his song clean through me.
Now comes night, hushing the lark in's furrow,
And the rain falls fine.
What have I done with what was dearest to me?

Thatch and wick, fagot, and tea on trivet,—
These and more it was; it was all my cheer.
Now comes night, smelling of box and privet,
And the rain falls fine.
Have I left it out in the rain?—It is not here.

PUEBLO POT

THERE as I bent above the broken pot from the
    mesa pueblo,
Mournfully many times its patterned shards piecing
    together and laying aside,
Appeared upon the house-top, two Navajos en-
    chanted, the red-shafted flicker and his bride,
And stepped with lovely stride
To the pergola, flashing the wonder of their under-
    wings;
There stood, mysterious and harsh and sleek,
Wrenching the indigo berry from the shedding
    woodbine with strong ebony beak.

His head without a crest
Wore the red full moon for crown;
The black new moon was crescent on the breast
Of each;
From the bodies of both a visible heat beat down,
And from the motion of their necks a shadow
    would fly and fall,
Skimming the court and in the yellow adobe wall
Cleaving a blue breach.

Powerful was the beauty of these birds.
It boomed like a struck bell in the silence deep
    and hot.

I stooped above the shattered clay; passionately I
        cried to the beauty of these birds,
"Solace the broken pot!"

The beauty of these birds
Opened its lips to speak;
Colours were its words,
The scarlet shaft on the grey cheek,
The purple berry in the ebony beak.
It said, "I cannot console
The broken thing; I can only make it whole."

Wisdom, heretic flower, I was ever afraid
Of your large, cool petals without scent!
Shocked, betrayed,
I turned to the comfort of grief, I bent
Above the lovely shards.
But their colours had faded in the fierce light of
        the birds.
And as for the birds, they were gone. As suddenly
        as they had come, they went.

WHEN CAESAR FELL

When Caesar fell, where yellow Tiber rolls
   Its heavy waters muddy,
Life, that was ebbing from a hundred holes
   In Caesar's body,
Cried with a hundred voices to the common air,
   The unimperial day,
"Gather me up, oh, pour me into the veins of even
    a gilder of hair!
   Let me not vanish away!"

The teeth of Caesar at the ignoble word
   Were ground together in pride;
No sound came from his lips: the world has heard
   How Caesar died.
In the Roman dust the cry of Caesar's blood
   Was heard and heard without wonder
Only by the fly that swam in the red flood
   Till his head went under.

LETHE

Ah, drink again
This river that is the taker-away of pain,
And the giver-back of beauty!

In these cool waves
What can be lost?—
Only the sorry cost
Of the lovely thing, ah, never the thing itself!

The level flood that laves
The hot brow
And the stiff shoulder
Is at our temples now.

Gone is the fever,
But not into the river;
Melted the frozen pride,
But the tranquil tide
Runs never the warmer for this,
Never the colder.

Immerse the dream.
Drench the kiss.
Dip the song in the stream.

ON FIRST HAVING HEARD
THE SKYLARK

NOT knowing he rose from earth, not having seen
    him rise,
Not knowing the fallow furrow was his home,
And that high wing, untouchable, untainted,
A wing of earth, with the warm loam
Closely acquainted,
I shuddered at his cry and caught my heart.
Relentless out of heaven his sweet crying like a
    crystal dart
Was launched against me. Scanning the empty sky
I stood with thrown-back head until the world
    reeled.
Still, still he sped his unappeasable shafts against
    my breast without a shield.
He cried forever from his unseen throat
Between me and the sun.
He would not end his singing, he would not have
    done.
"Serene and pitiless note, whence, whence are you?"
I cried. "Alas, these arrows, how fast they fall!
Ay, me, beset by angels in unequal fight,
Alone high on the shaven down surprised, and not
    a tree in sight!"

Even as I spoke he was revealed
Above me in the bright air,
A dark articulate atom in the mute enormous
blue,
A mortal bird, flying and singing in the morning
there.
Even as I spoke I spied him, and I knew,
And called him by his name;
"Blithe Spirit!" I cried. Transfixed by more than
mortal spears
I fell; I lay among the foreign daisies pink and
small,
And wept, staining their innocent faces with fast-
flowing tears.

TO A MUSICIAN

Who, now, when evening darkens the water and
  the stream is dull,
Slowly, in a delicate frock, with her leghorn hat in
  her hand,
At your side from under the golden osiers moves,
Faintly smiling, shattered by the charm of your
  voice?

There, today, as in the days when I knew you well,
The willow sheds upon the stream its narrow leaves,
And the quiet flowing of the water and its faint smell
Are balm to the heart that grieves.

Together with the sharp discomfort of loving you,
Ineffable you, so lovely and so aloof,
There is laid upon the spirit the calmness of the
  river view:
Together they fall, the pain and its reproof.

Who, now, under the yellow willows at the water's
  edge
Closes defeated lips upon the trivial word unspoken,
And lifts her soft eyes freighted with a heavy pledge
To your eyes empty of pledges, even of pledges
  broken?

PART FOUR

SONNET

Life, were thy pains as are the pains of hell,
So hardly to be borne, yet to be borne,
And all thy boughs more grim with wasp and thorn
Than armoured bough stood ever; too chill to spell
With the warm tongue, and sharp with broken
    shell
Thy ways, whereby in wincing haste forlorn
The desperate foot must travel, blind and torn,
Yet must I cry,—So be it; it is well.

So fair to me thy vineyards, nor less fair
Than the sweet heaven my fathers hoped to gain;
So bright this earthly blossom spiked with care,
This harvest hung behind the boughs of pain,
Needs must I gather, guessing by the stain
I bleed, but know not wherefore, know not where.

SONNET

Grow not too high, grow not too far from home,
Green tree, whose roots are in the granite's face!
Taller than silver spire or golden dome
A tree may grow above its earthy place,
And taller than a cloud, but not so tall
The root may not be mother to the stem,
Lifting rich plenty, though the rivers fall,
To the cold sunny leaves to nourish them.
Have done with blossoms for a time, be bare;
Split rock; plunge downward; take heroic soil;
Deeper than bones—no pasture for you there;
Deeper than water, deeper than gold and oil:
Earth's fiery core alone can feed the bough
That blooms between Orion and the Plough.

SONNET TO GATH

Country of hunchbacks!—where the strong,
    straight spine,
Jeered at by crooked children, makes his way
Through by-streets at the kindest hour of day,
Till he deplore his stature, and incline
To measure manhood with a gibbous line;
Till out of loneliness, being flawed with clay,
He stoop into his neighbour's house and say,
"Your roof is low for me—the fault is mine."

Dust in an urn long since, dispersed and dead
Is great Apollo; and the happier he;
Since who amongst you all would lift a head
At a god's radiance on the mean door-tree,
Saving to run and hide your dates and bread,
And cluck your children in about your knee?

THE PIONEER

On the Unveiling of a Statue to Lucretia Mott,
Susan B. Anthony, and Elizabeth Cady Stanton.
Washington, November eighteenth, 1923.

Upon this marble bust that is not I
Lay the round, formal wreath that is not fame;
But in the forum of my silenced cry
Root ye the living tree whose sap is flame.
I, that was proud and valiant, am no more;—
Save as a dream that wanders wide and late,
Save as a wind that rattles the stout door,
Troubling the ashes in the sheltered grate.
The stone will perish; I shall be twice dust.
Only my standard on a taken hill
Can cheat the mildew and the red-brown rust
And make immortal my adventurous will.
    Even now the silk is tugging at the staff:
    Take up the song; forget the epitaph.

TO JESUS ON HIS BIRTHDAY

For this your mother sweated in the cold,
For this you bled upon the bitter tree:
A yard of tinsel ribbon bought and sold;
A paper wreath; a day at home for me.
The merry bells ring out, the people kneel;
Up goes the man of God before the crowd;
With voice of honey and with eyes of steel
He drones your humble gospel to the proud.
Nobody listens. Less than the wind that blows
Are all your words to us you died to save.
O Prince of Peace! O Sharon's dewy Rose!
How mute you lie within your vaulted grave.
  The stone the angel rolled away with tears
  Is back upon your mouth these thousand years.

SONNET

Not that it matters, not that my heart's cry
Is potent to deflect our common doom,
Or bind to truce in this ambiguous room
The planets of the atom as they ply;
But only to record that you and I,
Like thieves that scratch the jewels from a tomb,
Have gathered delicate love in hardy bloom
Close under Chaos,—I rise to testify.
This is my testament: that we are taken;
Our colours are as clouds before the wind;
Yet for a moment stood the foe forsaken,
Eyeing Love's favour to our helmet pinned;
Death is our master,—but his seat is shaken;
He rides victorious,—but his ranks are thinned.

ON HEARING A SYMPHONY OF
BEETHOVEN

Sweet sounds, oh, beautiful music, do not cease!
Reject me not into the world again.
With you alone is excellence and peace,
Mankind made plausible, his purpose plain.
Enchanted in your air benign and shrewd,
With limbs a-sprawl and empty faces pale,
The spiteful and the stingy and the rude
Sleep like the scullions in the fairy-tale.
This moment is the best the world can give:
The tranquil blossom on the tortured stem.
Reject me not, sweet sounds! oh, let me live,
Till Doom espy my towers and scatter them.
A city spell-bound under the aging sun,
Music my rampart, and my only one.